Things I Can't Say In Prose

Poems

by

CHARLIE W. STARR

ISBN: 978-1-959544-19-7

Wootton Major Publishing
Austin, TX

Cover art by Becky Starr
Author photo by Alli Mullikin

Interior art by Adobe Firefly & Wootton Major Publishing

www.woottonmajorpublishing.com

to Devin Brown

Table of Illustrations

Table of Contents

Incarnational

Comically Considered

Wrestling

About the Author

Preface

But for some business transactions posted on clay tablets in Mesopotamia, poetry is older than prose. The earliest stories we told, epics, were written in poetic verse. Then besides telling stories about great heroes, we started making confessions about ourselves. This we did in psalms and dithyrambs which eventually became the lyric poems and songs we make today. Poetry is ancient and so signals an archaic mode of thought—something still a part of us lying deep within, something which, because of who we are, means that *some things* cannot be said in any way except through poems.

If we look at our lives as analogs to a film, we can imagine hitting the pause button and projecting a single moment of time for others to see on a screen. That moment, so profound, so large in its scope—every thought, feeling, object, place and action of that moment—is captured in what Wordsworth called the "narrow confines" of poetry. There the timeless moment frozen in time can be expurgated from the self, expressed to others, and examined by those looking to see if any fellow travelers have thought, felt, experienced the same *things* that they have.

—Charlie W. Starr
November, 2024

Pain

&

Wishes

Why Red Bird Sings

He'd been there since '53
Most didn't know his real name
In the interview
(He sat in front of the tripod
A cigarette in his hand)
I asked him where he got the name "Red Bird"
He said when he was young
He used to practice
What his folks taught him
In the old folk tale:
If you see a red bird
Close your eyes and make a wish
If you can still see him
When you open your eyes
Your wish'll come true

And so I tried it
(Beside the tripod)
But when I opened my eyes
The wish hadn't come true
There he was, still
He wasn't due for parole
For another ten years

This is Not a Message

Staring at a picture on the wall...

Tear stained cheek
Glistens
Sunset through
The beveled glass window
Prism corners refracting
Staining walls,
Pictures
With ephemeral rainbows

He is blind to it
Like the eyes of her face
In the family picture
Look without seeing
Forever

It is an Image

Taking Trash

The dumpster
is at the end of an asphalt parking lot
black and glistening wet in lamp light
The plastic bags are heavy
and cumbersome

Night is misting fifty degrees
The droplets on my face
cold and sharp
Tinkerbell kisses
stings of anemic mosquitos
Trash is a serious business

There is always plenty for me

My feet are in high-tops
purple and whitely new
on the second load
The neighborhood is possessed:
There's a demon
I've felt him

Even now by the cars without names
he makes me think of
I can't say what...

> *I bend my face close to*
> *the page and the words*
> *are 3-D images coming*
> *to life on a TV screen*
> *written by a hand that*
> *doesn't look like it's*
> *attached to me*
> *But I feel it unlike my*
> *TV screen—*
> *You can't feel it when*

someone else takes
out the trash Too much
TV is a little death
too many glows above
dead cars with no names

...can't say it
for the fear
Fear is dying too
I can't say
when the trash is
heaping up on me
"I can't carry anymore"
No one sees
(what the demon sees)
me die a little more
when Chaos' sons
trade my affections

Trash is serious business

Texas Snow at 9:45 a.m.

Exam week

In fifteen minutes the first one done
The bell will ring and in they'll come—
But outside,
It is snowing

Now it is quiet;
I can sit by the heater
In a plastic yellow chair
In a drab yellow room
And watch the snow fall outside
On the parking lot:

Row after row of this model or that:
The suburban with the
Country radio station bumper sticker
The white VW bug painted with
Large hippie flowers:
Blue, orange, purple, red.
An old man in mostly yellow
Plaid pants, red scarf and leather jacket
Shuffles from the door puffing
Cigarette smoky, cold steaming breath
Walking to his car
Driving to his post as
Parking lot attendant.

Across the street
St. Barnabas's cathedral roof and
Pillared walkway rest
White/grey serene
Like a mausoleum,
But not deathly austere.

His heater belches steam
Like the plaid man,
Tries to shake off the snow,
White, yellow-white snow.

Snowflakes turn to rain as they
Splash to the ground
Rain drops which, for a moment,
Wanted to take their time
Coming down.

Up close, they fall lightly,
Gentle and slow,
But focus on the distance
The fall is a torrent, like rain.
The former seems more real,
More personal,
Not like watching from a window
In the cafeteria;
The latter, though,
Has more power.
Whether near or far,
The other side of the glass
Is silent.
Snow ought to be.
The quiet serene sound without,
Contrasts the noise of
Cafeteria workers within:
Running water, pressured for time
Cold snap of the walk-in cooler latch
Inharmonious clang of pots
Cackle of voices.

I turn to notice the few kids waiting here
A reminder that snow can be dreamy,
Dreams, escapist;
Reminded of the raucous

Hopes and dreams
Coming through
Those yellowed wood doors
Two minutes from now
When I have to turn to work.
But for now there's the snow...

The old man with mostly yellow pants
Decides it's better
To come in out of the cold
As the ten o'clock bell rings.

Emergency Rememory

Jesus reminded me
When I took Jana
To the emergency room
Her slightly separated shoulder
Making her think about crying
Making her stretch out her arm
In the position the X ray demanded
Wrapping her
In hospital clothes
Lying behind the curtain
Purple socks and shin guards
Still on her feet
Reminded me when they
Brought in the messy haired
Beer bellied nice enough man
Softball shirt stained
With the blood from his head
Where the ball had cracked his nose
Puffed his eye
Turned his features into some
Impossible Mardi Gras visage
When the woman in her late fifties
Came walking sedately through
The double glass doors
Purse between her hands
A stare of calm disbelief
(As she explains with a
Southern gentlewoman's accent)
Above her woolen black coat–
A full-length been-in-
the-closet-since-the-50s
Charcoal fabric (the heavy
Tweed match your couch cushions
Kind):

Standing calmly at the window
Blood on her golf ball swollen
Brow where she had fallen
On the stone steps
That eye red drowning white
And teary
But she didn't cry
Reminded as they sat her down
To check her in
Check her insurance
While her husband hobbled up
On a cane and broken-ankle-
Walking-boot
Too old to grieve with passion
Too hearted to hide the compassion
In his eyes
I was reminded waiting in the
Waiting area
Trying to keep my four-year-old
Entertained (under control)
Wondering at this job I'd got myself
Wandering over the lost passion
Dreams surrendered
Because soccer season
Paper grading
Family raising
Didn't allow the time–
Drifting in my
Romantic's
Lamenting
Passion
I was reminded of the
Compassion of the
Cross

He reminded me that
Reality is never second best

Wishes come true
Are more matters of surrender
Than fulfillment

That what
He did was no picnic
No poem
No Eros
His was an act of passion
Which He has no desire to repeat
Through my forgetting Heart

A Violation of Senses

Voices fire the shattered sound:
Synthetic echoes; a meticulous disarray.
Rising young stars? No, dreamers—who, parting,
Can't but love against their will,
Dreams unfulfilled.
Guitar case latch closed.

Fire lights the shattered sight—
Fluttering picture haze; child in a sleepless bed.
Twinkling stars: brief calm till the breaking:
Angry shouts (not death) do part,
Vows betrayed.
Tear stained pillow.

Light speaks: the shattered moon,
Half in darkness where He prays.
Flickering stars—no, torches approaching.
Here love is at its most intense,
Betrayal its deepest.
"With a kiss?"

Apoc-elipsis

It was a dream.
Night.
Standing in the backyard:
Giant mulberry
Back-tingle visible
In the shadow behind me;
Giant bushes
Peripheral shadows before.
Stars in the clear sky above—
More than you should
Be able to see
In the city,
More than my backyard.
They began to flash
Photo flashes of a
Frantic press capturing Madonna,
Light filling the sky.
Then from each star,
Waves of light like an
Aurora Borealis—
Radiating out of their glory
But not in concentric circles:
Sunlight on soapy water,
Moonlight on muddy pools
In which someone
Has spilled gasoline;
Wave overlapping waves.
Then the figure:
Outline in neon,
Stars and night visible through it,
Robed man with
Flowing light hair.
No question—
No question Who:

I felt the joy,
No question.
But if there were,
His name flashed in
Neon letters below
His invisible feet.

It lasted for a second.
It was enough
To feel the joy,
To know I had seen it.
To be filled with conviction
Fundamentalist sure

Allusions

Balance

Did Enkidu know what he was doing
When he left the harlot from the city
For the city,
Know what he was rushing to protect
What he'd had
When resting at her feet,
What he surrendered
When Gilgamesh finally threw him
To the ground?

Every morning
Husbands kiss their wives
(Who have to "run to the store today"),
Drive to work
Wondering why the here-we-go-again,
Maybe take a look
At the little frame on the desk
The white gown wedding picture,
And have that report on their boss's desk
By five.

Planting the Oar

I

In his eye, light burned
Nine fathoms deep.
In the moonless night center,
Thought I, something squirmed.

For me he did not stop.
Walked on in his grey rags:
Shabby, tattered, gossamer webs
Clinging to his skeleton frame.

But him I followed
Leaning hard on his stick
Under the weight
Of something heavier than sin.

And his head, smooth
Rain-baptized clean
And beard, white/grey
Like glacial ice floating
In a fog filled sea.

Followed I his refusal
To dine or drink or rest his limbs
Corpse-life-walking; nor even
The repast of a moment's human company.

And then surrendering Pretense:

VII

I followed down Kirk street
Till his fire-eye latched on
Old Marv Heiner—I know him—
Like a giant, white bird piercing its prey.

Old Marv, he stood watering
The same spot on his lawn
Listening to the old man's pitch
And me shouting down the sidewalk,

"Hey, what gives?!"
Marv dropped dead–
The old man turning red
Facing me
The sun setting on my back.

Crying his eyes out
Weeping some lover's joy
While I CPR'd the sinking corpse
Shouting down the sidewalk,
"Nine-one-one, call nine-one-one!"

Crying his heart blood loose:
"I hadn't to finish the story!"
Somehow, the fright in
Old Marv's face seemed peaceful.

When the ambulance came,
I followed the direction I thought he went,
But there wasn't anything
Except one unusual report:

Out at the old cemetery
A freshly dug grave out of plot
As if someone snuck in and dug
And buried who knows what.

Only the shovel stuck in the earth
Filled the duty of a marker.

Coming

Odysseus was planting the oar
And the children of Aeneas
Forgetting their father's ideals
For a vision of empire
Divining power without purpose.

On the holy mountain
Zeus considered how a
New name sounded
On Apollo's lyre
(He was down to three or four choices).

Meanwhile, outside the city of David,
A lumbering lion-man
Slouched its way toward Sinai,
In its stony face a contented bemusement:
What pleasure to finally sleep.

And in the waiting room of Olympus
An Akkadian deity named Baal
Impatiently thumb twiddles
For an audience to reveal Prometheus' secret:
The child to come, bringing death from Uruk to Asgard.

On Cavafy's "Ithaca"

I

Not really wanting to take his advice,
I nevertheless took my time getting to Ithaca.

I spent the first day at JFK on weather delay,
Wandering among bookstore shelves
Eating high priced, low nutrition airport food
And watching people read *Harry Potter*
And *The da Vinci Code* (not a decent book in sight)
Or play Sudoku or cell phone video games.

At Heathrow I realized I'd made my first island.
The woman at the ticket counter—her name was Polly—
Had a Cyclops's narrow vision
Regardless of diminutive size.
While I stared at a rotating billboard
Advertising safe sex on one side
(that made me think of Trojans)
And a car on the other
(I'm pretty sure it was a Lotus)
The muzack lulled me happily to sleep.
I missed my connection.

When I finally got to Ithaca—
Ten days late (though it felt like ten years)—
Athena, knowing the rigors of jet lag,
Shed over me a gentle sleep—
I didn't wake up for a day and a half.

Then it was time to go to the airport—
My two-week vacation was over.

II

If Cavafy is right, then of course Ithaca will disappoint.
But maybe the only reason the journey matters at all
Is because it is filled with tiny islands of destination along the way:
The hope of getting
to explore a cave
or listen to a good all-woman band
to win the Phyakian lottery
or get laid by a goddess.
But what good's a treasure (or bragging rights)
If you can't, finally, someday, make it home?

Ithaca never disappoints

Anachronisms

Arthur stood at the window pane
watching as the carriage pulled away
confident that his trusted friend
would carry his beloved wife
safely to London.
The clock chimed 9 a.m.

On the battlements,
Saxon Arthur and his band
watched from the walls
with their longbows in hand.

In the evening,
after the feast's good china
had been collected and washed,
Merlin climbed to his laboratory
in the high tower
pulled out his telescope
and recorded the orbit of Neptune
on spreadsheets he intended
to publish in print through
none other than Caxton himself.

Arthur, in his bedroom,
flipped the switch that lit the torches
and climbed beneath the sheets
oblivious to the danger he'd put
his nation in.
"Lance will be fine," he thought.
"It's Gwen I worry about."
And he thought of the Bard:
"Frailty, thy name is woman."
And as he drifted off to sleep:
"Who better than the strongest of men
to watch over her."

Ophelia

She couldn't,
Couldn't possibly understand
The workings of his mind.
Wasn't he a prince?

Imprints
That's what he left
On the hand, invisible
Staring there
Unremovably sticky
Dirty there
Removing any sight
Of pristine qualities.

Can't blame him
Can't blame him
And father busying about

> *Trying to protect*
> *His baby girl*
> *Scurrying about*
> *Behind curtains*
> *Peeping in*
> *Peeping in*
> *In on his baby girl*
> *On and in*
> *Why can't babies*
> *Stay little forever?*

Priceless possession
Of an old father's care
Looking for no price
But a place to set her
Thinking, "Is he not the prince?"
And hoping
Behind the curtains

To be always near
Near enough
Near enough

Who couldn't forgive—
His father newly dead
Something haunting his eyes—
It's the principle.

    And in the end
    It wasn't the madness
    Desiring company

Not the ponderous
Choice not to be
Nor even the
Crack about the convent
(Becoming a sister would've
Been easy for one so chaste
If only not for the father
Chastening her
Awakening in her
The forever-need
At night
Coming to
From behind
The curtain);

    In the end
    It was the
    Inviting thought—

Staring back
From beneath
The reflection—
To be
Finally,
Principally
Washed clean

Philo and Miso

Lost was Lewis,   lacking knowledge.
Tales of pagans   Tolkien taught
And Deus Divine   the dead reviving:
God of grace   salvation giving.
Jack thought myths   made factless musings,
sighs of *Sehnsucht*   breathed through silver.
With them Dyson   went late walking,
winding river's   windless wandering:
Addison's island,   idly roaming,
myths and meaning   made them ponder.
Suddenly silenced,   stunned to stopping
in their tracks,   the time breath-taking.
Wind arose there   waking wonder,
breath unlocking   understanding:
"Myth's *Invention*,   imitates image.
Trees are trees   in tellings versed.
None see stars   till silver living
Flame afire in   flow'ring love bursts.
Sub-creator,   source of Stories,
wakes the world,   makes *Wonder* mean.
Myth's the truth: we make it matter.
Christ's the myth,   the truth made fact.
Faith the fact,   no falsehood feigning,
Make the myth   your heart's new mind."

Ramifications

Some nights Digory would
wake up weeping–
Weeping for the destruction
he brought to
The land, a thousand
thousand years of
suffering in his single
lifetime all for
adventure and a bell:
For the hundred
years of winter in
a White Queen's
whim; for a Stone
slab and sharp
stone knife and his
master dead when
an apple tree was
no longer enough;
for Caspian's old aged
loneliness and wood
women cleaved in two:
A thousand, thousand
years of suffering in
his single lifetime.

On such nights he'd
wonder through the
old house, later the
comfortable little cottage,
always ending up in
the same room
a big wooden closet
standing against a
wall: carved and stained
by hand "stained by my hands"
he'd think, staring

at doors there
was no need
to try and open.

On such nights
in that place he'd
shed quiet tears
And a face at
the top of
the closet turns gold
and brown,
baptizes the wooden floor
with great big
splashes, one for each
of Professor Digory's.

On such nights he
finds himself falling
into sleep on the
stained wooden floor.

On the morning after
such nights, Digory
would wake with His
voice still ringing
in his ears: "Forgiveness
doesn't always mean solace."

And Digory would
go to his breakfast,
go to his work,
go to his books
forgiven and weeping.

Escapism

Susan thought it was tragic.
No, really:
She cried bitter tears
and on first hearing
in the shock of disbelief
wanted desperately
to turn to Aslan
and ask him why.
But then she remembered:
That had only been a game,
a fantasy played by four children
and an eccentric old don
all dead now,
all but Susan,
who never liked trains
and was coming to like animals
less and less.
Susan asked no one.
Games were for children,
and it didn't occur to her
that there might be someone
an adult could ask.
No.
Susan gave up questions.
And after a while
she gave up tears,
and pain,
and wondering,
and, instead, busied herself
with answers,
and friends,
and parties,
and marriage,
and children,
and a zest for her
day dreamy life–
      the only one she would ever know.

Juxta
positions

Flying

There's a white noise sound
Accompanying that smell
Peculiar to all commercial airliners
Unlike that of any home or
Office air conditioner:
High pitched
And more airy
Symbolic, I suppose
Of the machine's purpose.
Pavlov is engendered
In the frequent flier
The moment it hits the ear:
Motivation to swallow hard,
Gapingly yawn,
Hold the nose and blow;
Anything to equalize pressure.
Chilly artificial air
Can be augmented by the twist
Of an overhead dial,
A new soundlessness
Rushing out to harmonize with its sibling,
Together with humming jets'
Basso vibration,
Joining in quartet with air
Passing over fuselage
A white symphony for the ears'
Sense of sleep.

Flying is for the hearing.
It isn't for sight
Only the pilots can see ahead;
Not for taste
Or else airline food would be
Satirized less;
Touch? More like touchlessness
"White touch" if you will.
More, recline-the-chair-back,

Grab-a-midget-pillow, pull-
The-window-shade sleep appeal
(Unless the cabin's crowded
And the seats don't go back
Or can't because the man
Behind has legs too long for
His space)–definitely
Not for touch.
Smell sniffs for itself.

Sight drifts away
As the plane lifts upward,
Image of the flight attendant's
Semaphore dance inside the lids,
Waking to the screech of tires on concrete,
Air brakes roaring their
Demand for reversal.
The high pitched hissing
Says goodbye
With a step onto the concourse.

He rubs his forelegs together
In relish of the all you can eat
Buffet before him,
The pungent odor drawing
With a drive
Like an animal in heat.
Then a swoosh sounding
Rush of air sends him flying
Instinctively backwards.
Something fleshy-tan looming
Large and swift before his eyeses
The multifaceted perspective
Increases the horror of the
Moment a thousand times;
The ubiquitous buzzing
Behind him, present
Not since birth but since
Being borne upon the atmosphere,

Is a comforting green light
For his sense of survival.
He alights again only to have
His dinner interrupted again.
A few more tries convinces him
Of the futility.
He moves on.
This strange cylinder world
Into which he has flown
Has too many noises,
And he doesn't understand
What invisible barrier
Keeps him from getting through
To the bright sun and blue sky
To which he has risen so high.

And he doesn't understand why
His comforting buzz provokes
The instinct to shew
In the large, looming fleshy-tans.

Does he know?
Does he realize that the praxis
His race accomplishes so well,
The thing for which they're named
That he has achieved a
Thousand times more height,
Distance and speed
Than any of his brothers
Could ever dream?
Does he know when he follows
The others onto the concourse,
That he has become
Johnathan Livingstone Fly?
And did the big French Woman
In the Paris bakery know,
When she swatted him,
That he was an American?
That he was the savior of his race?

Show and Tell

Nikki shook the little butterfly
in the jar
showing her preschool friends
it was still alive
They all watched eagerly
at the windows
As she and I walked outside
to let it go
But whether from exhaustion
or asphyxiation
or starvation or shake-jarring
injury it just lay
there beating a helpless wing
against the sidewalk
And the faces in the window
didn't understand how
deep was their disappointment
Miss Phyllis placed it
mercifully on the grass to die
and Nikki and I
went inside for circle time
While they sang
I thought of evil death and
Eden wondered about
murder at the hand of an
innocent at the
cruelty of benevolence and
the egocentric
impulse of happy children
to show and tell

What can it possibly have been like
To be Melville
Thirty years
Thirty years in a customs house

Reduced to files and forms
Thirty years after writing
The American Masterpiece
And everyone missed it
And you started to believe that
They were right
What when a man
In his prime
To have soared intuitive heights
Sailing forever exiled waters
Thirty years

Reduced to an occasional
Poetic scribble
And nothing left but cynicism
Family estrangement
Pain
It's a wonder he didn't
Throw up his hands
And sound a mighty whimper
"I would prefer not to
Go on living today"
Oh Herman
Oh Me
How close to the rubbish heap
Was that manuscript
They found in your desk drawer
And you to obscurity
Till the roaring twenties
When a mousy voice
In a University somewhere
Said, "Hey wait a minute"

Dying

He was warm and safe and
Well, not dry.
Floating in that
Perfect watery world,
Rolling about in
The uniform bath
The temperature right
From head to toe
(Or toe to head,
Depending)
Never having a stomach groan
Never having to ask
Hooked up to that
Tube.
Twilight world
Of restful sleep
Perchance to dream
All day.
No wonder, when the
Convulsions began
When he was pressed
Through the canal
Out into painful light
The enraptured faces
Of mom and dad
Blurry in the blindness
Brilliant before him
No wonder he cried,
Wailing like a newborn baby.

They kept enough blankets on him
The bed, firm and comfortable,
But the cooling sweat
Poring out
Demanded the hassle

The pain of changing his bed clothes
And a stale smell
Of something somewhere
Between being alive
And not
Floating all around
And the sound of wheeze
And rasp beeping
Mechanically
Hooked up to that
Tube.
And pain killer enough
To keep his murky
Consciousness free
From blinding
Full awareness
Agony.
No wonder,
When the seizure began
And the monitor flat lined
His body vomiting
Him out into
Brightness too intense
To do anything
But soothe,
The rapture
More erotic
Than romance,
No wonder he cried
Weeping like a newborn baby.

Sun Worship

The Atchafalaya Swamp Bridge
(Lafayette to Baton Rouge)

Those who think "watery grave" a cliche
have never seen the
sparsely dense stumps
of trees
in these swamps below
when dawn is just
a yellow-pale coronet on the
white and grey and black
of the water.
The single collection of
these solitary tombstones
(in this state where the dead
are buried above ground
because there's water
six feet below)
preminisces the magic
of the eerie mists rising
(just down the road)
from the clear crystal
clouded by its own life
mists meeting the sun's
first rays bending its
straight light into something
you never thought you'd see:
horizontal sunbeams.

On Campus
(In Eastern Kentucky)

The sun is behind the hill
behind the college
(behind which is the road

44

I walk to my house)
but not set so much
that it still can't light
the cloud studded blue
sky from underneath.
The clouds are orange and
gold, a paler yellow highlighting
the shallowing blue
(but not so shallow as
not to be blue),
and for a minute I think
I see but for the flatlessness
a sunset from home
here in the October air
chilled in just that certain way
that Texans don't know enough
about cold to know how to describe.
Except for the one dark cloud
above me sprinkling giant
flakes of snow
(only a few here and there:
frozen wisps of air)
flakes like down feathers
falling from an orange/blue sky,
and the only thing that could
make this sunset more perfect
would be to actually see the sun
fall behind the earth.
But then I think that taking
the hill away would change
the light completely,
ruining the effect,
and I chalk the impulse up
to homesickness as I stop
to put my briefcase down
and button up my coat.

Incarnational

Thanksgiving in Deweyville

Willows weep over swamp land
Beside the potted asphalt road,
On the other side of the driveway,
Running through the yard, where
You have to step around little
Grey, bumpy-built crawdad mounds.
The air is wet and musty with
The fullness of Louisiana life
In my nose
(So much Louisiana that it's
A shame it got stuck on the
Texas side and perhaps
Even a bit ashamed).
Makes me drowsy.
Makes me want to hit that
Old comfy couch for a nap
Before the turkey and gumbo
Are even served.

Nanny and "Aint" Kitty
Are popsicle twins
In their pastel peach
And blue sweatsuits,
Speaking with husky
Cigarette voices, saying,
"Yeah" with two Southern
Syllables, hugging with
Little pats on the back:
"Wayll, Chorley! How R Yuuuue?"

Howard makes sure,
Holding Tyrel's and "Trishy's" hands,
We ask a blessing for the meal.
He's deeper than the swamp;
He's Nanny's son.
Margie's her daughter,

Who makes it every year
Even when J.C. has to
Work the refinery night shift
(He manages to make it
Just about every year anyway),
Bringing the kids along
If they don't sleep till noon
And drive themselves:

Pat, the college football player
Turned security guard,
Knows enough to hide his big
Teddy bear heart on the job.
We know enough
To look at the smile
Not his size.
Heather, the awkward little eighth grader
In glasses, has been stolen and replaced
By a lovely young homecoming queen
The pre-teen shape turned shapely
Excited about going to college.

Help yourself in the kitchen
To turkey, stuffing & sweet potatoes;
Fresh fried shrimp, rice &
Seafood gumbo. But I don't
Eat much gumbo
Don't like to dig the crab meat
Out of the shells.
Round one at the table:
Me, Becky, the kids
(Bryan my son always wants
Twice as much Ketchup as he needs),
And Miss Wilda
Who I finally learned was
J.C.'s mom, moved down South
To be with family,
To find out this isn't
Kansas anymore.

Howard and I have talked about
What's going on at their little church,
What I'm going to be teaching
In Sunday school
By the time we settle on
The reclining chair or
The comfy couch,
Settle in to watch the
Cowboys play.
Becky, more comfortable here
Than at our house,
Laughs with her mom at
Something that was funny
When she was in high school.
Pat (Trishy actually Patricia
It's a versatile name

When country folk get a hold of it)
Is glad her daughter, my wife,
Is home. She and "Beck" make
Plans to hit every Wal-Mart
In a hundred mile radius
For tomorrow's first day of
Christmas shopping.
Mom's also glad to see me.
We think she likes me better
Than her own daughter.
Truth? I'm more comfortable
Here than at home, too.
Comfortable enough to drift
Down the bayou in the
Reclining chair,
Country woman cackle in my ears,
Oblivious to the score
Or time remaining in
The hazy rectangular
Glowing before me.

Autumn Toward Austin

Autumn on the Texas highways
Is twenty shades of dull.
We don't have the bright
Blazing colors of the North's
Leaf dying trees.

Our yellow brown embers
Do not catch the eye with brilliance,
Don't usurp the aesthetic will
And demand we look,
Demand we look.

So when you choose to
Notice the multiple shades of earth
On the hillside as you drive by,
It is an act of heroism
Not a glandular impulse.

Your reward is a lesson
In subtlety;
Shades of meaning become
More concrete
Than ever before.

Research Papers on Saturday Afternoon

The front came through at about 6:00
Dropping rain and hail
In a one block radius.
(Hamlet was dying on the VCR.)
By 6:30 it had ended
Along with my plans to mow.

The relieving breeze smelled
(through my stuffy nose)
Cool and fresh
Like the woods at church camp
But not so intense
Not in the city.

Till 7:00 the air was jaundiced,
Filled with yellow diffusion
Light but not just the sky
The air itself.
We opened the doors,
Turned the A.C. off.

The backyard jaundiced but
The front watched the
Front creep heavy dark
Black away
Bug light sky just
Following over the roof.

At 7:10 the sky was grey,
Sun dissipated by clouds
Now disappearing
Yellow street lights
Like beacons peering
Through the sliding glass door.
The baby's swing rocks
With the leaves,

The big back yard tree
A silhouette of arms reaching
Over the house, a touch of green
All that remains in the grass outside.

The moment leaves.
Mom screams dinner;
Baby just screams,
The rainy cool freshness on
My nose replaced by
Fried fish and vinegar.

7:20–the ceiling fan chain clicks
Against its base.
Front door shut,
Backyard a shadow,
I go back to grading papers,
'I am rewinding Horatio.'

Night School Over

This lot is cold
Walking on icy asphalt
Feet pounding my head
And a burden on my shoulder
A bag of precious papers
With which I've been too eager to part
Impart a word, a light.

Not like these lights
Cold and lightless
Lying a bit of sun
Just enough to grey-see
How far it is
Still to my car
Out of the
Windless cold
Like being dead
Or on the moon.

But the clouds are too
Thick for that
And these artificial stars
A hundred feet high
Remind me oppressively
How far away the
Real ones have removed
Themselves from us,
thinking, "They've got
their own lights now."

The clouds, you see,
Aren't natural.
We put them there;
They follow us
When we walk
Through cold

Parking lots
At ten
At night.

Dreams slung over my shoulder
Keys jingling
Between numbing
Grey fingers.

Refugee

Smajo* stands on the outskirts
of the various little church chats,
a placid my-English-isn't-quite-
good-enough-yet smile
mannequined to his face

But the leg was for the doctors to build—
a chunk of bone
piece of shoulder
skin graft
nine months
good as new (they say)

Leaning there on his crutches
Smajo smiles at my two year old
standing beside him staring
at the preschool toys being set up
in the sanctuary

I watch at a distance
He shifts to his good leg
shifts one crutch to the other hand
bends and points
and asks the obvious
(regardless of the language)
And holds out his hand

My daughter
takes his hand with trust
as if he were her other father
the one from Bosnia

I watch them walk

———————————————————
* *Pronounced Smĭ-yō*

hand in hand
from a distance
(too socially intimidated
to walk up and find out
how much I could talk to him
I think about my fear in shame
for thought of the fears
he must walk daily)

Holding her hand he bends
and limps
slowly
and she keeps double baby-step time
doesn't run
doesn't pull toward
or pull away–
hand in hand
a movie sur-reel
one moment
A carpenter from Sarajevo
places a little girl

on a little wooden seesaw
(the kind that rocks on crescent feet)
bends at the other end
and rocks her up and down
up and down
Is he thinking of the little girl
he saved from mortar fire
when his own thigh became
her life shield

In a moment
the moment passes
and Alli runs off
to a big plastic car

I watch, from the foyer
of a Christian church,

the Muslim refugee
who puts shame into my heart
for failing to walk over
and say, "Hello"

Looking at Orion Near Winter's End

The next time I see you
probably won't be
from Texas skies,

but that "faithful companion"
of yours will
keep you company.
He'll still be there
when I'm not.
When my life's done,
however long lived,
he'll still be there for you.

And hardly any time
will have passed
In dog-star years.

Comically Considered

Being Left Handed

Isn't bad because
    I can't use the scissors
    Put papers in the file folder right
    Keep my hand free from ink smudges when I write
    Open a new jar of peanut butter
    Sit comfortably in a school room desk

Isn't bad because
    I don't fall right in line
    Or think in a right frame of mind
    (In fact I do
    But if we're so much
    In our right minds,
    How come we can be so crazy)
    Or feel so left out
    Or agonize, guilty,
    Since right's true opposite is wrong
    (In fact there's hope
    Two wrongs don't make a right
    But three lefts do)

But, rather,
Because it leaves me
So completely vulnerable
To Cliché

Retentive

"Because I like to."
I like to pick my nose,
Like the sensation
Of freeing my nostrils
From the flotsam and jetsam
Barnacled to their sides,
The greasy gunk
Matted in among the hairs
(Sometimes you pull a few–
Making trimming easier in the morning).

How blessed is the man
Who inhales unencumbered.

"Of course not eat them."
That would be incestuous.
Each gets a rating on the
Crusty to Gooey scale,
And sometimes I imagine
Shapes for them
As you would do with clouds:
An ice cream cone,
A piece of driftwood,
A toothbrush.

No wonder it's called the Ol' factory
It produces so much–
Especially during allergy season.

"I don't hold to the Freudian, no."
Plunging into the orifice,
Digging and probing.

Something more:
Diving into mystery
The place of darkness;

Getting close
(As close as possible from the outside)
To the mind's core.
I like to keep in touch
With my thoughts,
With the primordial places,
Chasms of the past

Archetypes architecting
Our present,
Governed by what we
Do not see.

Only the courageous
Make the nose bloodying dive
To bring, breached,
Out in the open,
Truth.
Only the brave
And Egyptian morticians.

"In the car mostly."
Sometimes in the bathroom,
Near a kleenex,
Lying in bed,
Sitting watching T.V.
But I like it most
In the car,
Not bothering to wonder
What the people
In the next lane think.

When I crashed,
They pulled my finger
Out of my brain
With pliers.

Landscape with the Fall
of William Carlos Williams

According to Brueghel
when it all went to hell
it was spring

an overdressed farmer was slicing
an ice cream cake
the whole landscape

of the landscape painting
realizing it was more of a
seascape

the edge of the sea
and the rest of the sea
taking more canvas space
than the landscape itself

sweating in the sun
(this was the overdressed farmer)
that melted
the emperor's ice cream

Insignificantly
off the coast
there was

a splash quite unnoticed
this was
Eliot drowning

after I pushed him out of the plane
with a manuscript of all of e. e. cummings's
poems in his hands

Writer's Block

(A Poem)

by

Charlie W. Starr

Writer's Block

(II)

Nothing came to mind
When I sat to write.
So I write about nothing.
Of everything I've ever written,
Nothing lacked substance
The most
(Well almost–there were
A few lousy limericks).
Ask me what I wrote about today;
I'll proudly tell you:
Nothing.
At all.

Wrestling

Half Sarcastically

I would write much more poetry than I do
If I had the time
But I'm a sinner
Too busy keeping myself
Keeping my family alive
I'm too busy to be that prolific
Time to survive
Didn't you know that's why there's suffering?
Better little babies
Get tossed on bayonets
Than a man be idle enough
To lose his soul

Only Half

Theodicy

(Chapter four, Book five
The Brothers Karamazov)

And God said,
"Let Us make man in Our own Image."

And in His omniscient Imagination,
God beheld His free creation
And saw the evil perpetrated
By men
On man—
Saw parents defeating their children
Robbing their freedom
Walling them up in jars
In the corners of the house
In closets filled with excrement
In beds invaded
By sticky, wet daddies,
Babies torn from their
Living mother's wombs for sport
Tossed and caught
On bayonets for spite
Tempted with gun barrel
Pacifiers spit drooling
From mouth on metal
Before the trigger pulled,
Women writhing for the public pleasure
Pretzel positioned for Freudian fantasies,
Men of love burning the impious alive
Dislodging their bones crushing their feet
Feeding their eyes to the rats hacking off
Any part that offends in Jesus' name, Amen.

And God changed His mind—
He saw how "the fabric of
Human destiny" would find
It "essential to torture
To death one tiny creature."

And God changed His mind.

He did not make man—
    And cities were never built
    And sunsets never seen
    And lovers never embraced
    And this was never written
    And you never read it
    You never were.

Christmas 1

Did they know,
The people of that distant planet,
Building their cities,
Raising their young,
Making their monuments,
Laughing on patios in the
Evenings of nostalgic summers,
The scent of freshly cut
Grass in the air abuzz with
Friendly, firefly moths,
Viewing the landscapes on
Free museum walls,
Delighting in love making,
Eating juice-bursty fruit
On the lawn at an outdoor concert
On a planet knowing only peace
And beauty–
Did they know, when they died
That the light from their
Sun gone nova
Would guide those wanderers,
All these years later
To an experience they could
Best describe as
Satisfactory
(for the child here did not
come from Krypton)?
And in learning,
Did those who accepted
Assure reservations for themselves
In Jerusalem?
And how sparse is the population
Of the City so far?

Oasis

The desert grabs my throat
Like a vice grating my pipes;
I crawl on bloodied hands
Defying her lust for death.
And she laughs.
And I die.

A door opens in the desert,
A door that has no walls,
And I crawl through,
Defying the desert.
And this life's troubles
Are done.

At an oasis he gave in–
My brother drowned himself for thirst.
But I would not drop to my face
To lap up the water of life.

Now we are both dead,
And my troubles have just begun.
He, like a child, gave in.
I, like a man, crawled on.

And he rests at an oasis.
And I have come to a desert.

All That's Required

Interpret:

GODISNOWHERE

A Christmas Carol

"And it came about as her
soul was departing (for she died),
that she named him Ben-oni;
but his father called him Benjamin.
So Rachel died and was buried
on the way to Ephrath
(that is, Bethlehem)."

Genesis 35:18, 19

What did I care that he
renamed him?
For me he was "sorrow,"
though I was pleased to know,
as I lay there, spent,
numbness already spreading
from somewhere in my middle,
that I had given him
a son of remembrance
(no more surrogate shame)
to sit at his right hand,
remind him of what I had given
when there was still
such a long way to go...

"... Rachel died,
to my sorrow, in the land of
Canaan on the journey, when there
was still some distance to go
to Bethlehem."

Genesis 48:7

Fourteen years without her–
working to get her.
Fourteen years, and now
how many more without her?
Every day the boy reminds me

of the blessing and the curse
(more surely than a disjointed hip ever could).
And when I was sure
I had lost him and Joseph both,
I was sure the tears I shed
were hers.
For how could a man
weep so bitterly
at the loss of the young?

And how could either one of them know that her journey to
Bethlehem was yet two millennia away?

"Thus says the Lord,
'A voice is heard in Ramah,
Lamentation and bitter weeping.
Rachel is weeping for her children;
She refuses to be comforted for her children,
Because they are no more.'"

Jeremiah 31:15

Here were you, Lord,
jilted lover,
prodigal Father.
And Your child was a nation,
Your beloved a harlot,
Your prophet a tired old man
warning them and warning them
(You would not let me be silent);
and deaf were their ears,
and cold became my heart.
When was it ever written
that You chose prophets
prone to depression and
suicidal thoughts?
You in Your pain–
how did You ever put up with me?

The spirit of Rachel

is upon the land,
watching from the grave
as they ship Benjamin and David
to Babylon from a
weigh station that is
too poetically perfect.
May that spirit be
upon us all,
that we should not forget
to read the verse
that follows.

Finally, the journey to Bethlehem complete. Ground Zero, and a donkey, and no room in the inn. The Son of promise is born and this time the Mother lives. But when She departs for Egypt, she remains.

> "A voice was heard in Ramah,
> Weeping and great mourning,
> Rachel weeping for her children;
> And she refused to be comforted,
> Because they were no more."
>
> Matthew 2:18

I had to, don't you see?
I am King!
ME!
And I... will not share my kingdom
with a child.
More sons...
They can have m o r e, they–
They're constantly breeding,
(adding to the surplus population...)
Besides,
If–he–IS
this child of eh...
    prophecy,
then I am only an
instrument for the... the
fulfillment of Holy Writ.

Let history remember me
as it will.
If you're looking to cast blame,
lay it at the Penman's feet...

Did those mothers of Bethlehem ever find out why Herod did what he did? If they learned, three decades later, did it matter? Did they curse You or bless? Did they realize, in the spirit of Rachel, that with the one comes the other, that Ramah, five miles north and Bethlehem, five miles south were only half the distance in years to Jerusalem (Rachel's been waiting to go there all along)? I don't know.

I only know, two millennia later, that Rachel had one name for the child; Jacob had another.

THE END.

About the Author

Charlie W. Starr is a Professor of English and Humanities at Great Lakes Christian College, and a Professor of Inklings Studies at Northwind Seminary. He teaches, writes and lectures on the works of C. S. Lewis and J.R.R. Tolkien as well as teaching courses on literary classics and film. Charlie has published three books and numerous articles on Lewis along with over thirty never-before seen C. S. Lewis manuscripts and has been hailed as the world's leading expert on Lewis's handwriting.

Charlie also writes fiction and poetry, having published short stories, children's fantasy and three novels in a projected seven-book science fiction series called *The Tales of Solomon Star*: *The Heart of Light*, *The Darkening Time*, and *The Aurora Gambit* (soon to be re-released by FAEROS Publishing as *The Man of Light Saga*).

www.ingramcontent.com/pod-product-compliance
Lightning Source LLC
Chambersburg PA
CBHW021937040426
42448CB00008B/1112